Under Satan's Attack

Don Grendell, Th.D.

Under Satan's Attack
© 2011 by Don Grendell, Th.D.

ISBN-13: 978-1480177451

ISBN-10: 1480177458

First printing 2012

Printed in the United States of America

Scripture quotations taken from the King James Bible, Thompson Chain Reference, B.B. Kirkbride Bible Co., Inc. 1954,1964

All rights reserved. No part of this book may be reproduced or transmitted in any form or by any means, electronic or mechanical, including photocopying, recording, or by any information storage and retrieval system, without permission in writing from the copyright owner.

Firestarter Publications
firestarternow@yahoo.com
Huntsville, Arkansas 72740

DEDICATION

This book is dedicated to my wife, Mary, who not only stood by me during the attack on my ministry, but has done so for the last thirty years.

I also dedicate this to my son, Donnie, our daughter, Lisa, who have been such a blessing to our lives and who we saw grow spiritually during the ordeal.

Circle H Ministries
P. O. Box 1125
Morrillton, AR 72110

Contents

Chapter		Page
Chapter 2	My Calling to Childcare Work	7
Chapter 3	My Previous Callings	10
Chapter 4	Brief History of Circle H	15
Chapter 5	Our Stand on Licensing	20
Chapter 6	The Attack	24
Chapter 7	The Outcome	38
Chapter 8	How to Stop the Attacks	53
Chapter 9	Conclusion	57
Chapter 10	Sequel	59

Chapter 1

My Personal Testimony

I was not born into a Christian family; therefore, I was not raised in church. I went to Sunday School a few times and had attended only one worship service up to the time I was fifteen years of age. The only Christian training I received was from my Aunt Ella, who used to read Bible stories to my sister and I when we were young. I knew nothing of the experience of being "born again". I do not remember hearing the term used.

I came from a broken home, as my mother and father were divorced when I was four years old. We were left with my grand-parents, who took care of us until I was fifteen years old.

I remember the night my father and mother separated. They had a fight and mother left the house. We went to bed and the next morning I remember getting up and looking for my mother and dad; however, mother was not there. I looked up at dad and asked, "Daddy, where is Mommy?" He said, "Son mommy did not come home last night." That was the beginning of the end of their marriage. No one knows what you feel at a time like that, unless you have experienced it.

A few years ago while visiting with my dad he told me that mom did come home that night, but he was mad and wouldn't let her in the house. He has always regretted it since and took all the blame for the divorce. I had the privilege of winning my Dad to the Lord and seeing him healed. One of his legs was shorter than the other and we saw the Lord actually grow it out to the normal length.

I had joined the Air Force just before getting married. We were married in Steel Bridge Baptist Church in Lonoke, Arkansas August 16th 1958. Immediately after getting married I was shipped to Thule Greenland for a year. We spent our first year of married life apart from each other. We did have a 30 day leave to spend together before I left which was a blessing.

All of this took place before I attended church regularly. We were stationed in Mountain Home, Idaho, after I returned from Greenland in 1959. We had only been in church a few weeks when I realized something was wrong in my life. I talked to Rev. C.A. Thomas, pastor of Mountain Home Baptist Church. He shared the plan of salvation with me, and I invited Jesus into my life, was baptized and joined the church.

About a month after I was saved, I felt the Lord calling me into the ministry. This was a total surprise to me because I did not realize the Lord called people to preach. This was not easy, because I was a very bashful person. It scared me to death anytime I had to speak in front of a group, regardless how small. I was timid around my own family. I was so bashful, I would not even ask for food to be passed to me when we were eating. I would do without. If I had to stand up in class and say anything, I would break out in a cold sweat.

When the Lord called me to preach, I knew it was to a special ministry; however, I did not know what it was. I left the Air Force to go to college and prepare for what the Lord had in mind for my life.

While waiting for the Lord to show me what He wanted me to do, I accepted the pastorate of Douglasville First Baptist Church in Little Rock, Arkansas. We had a wonderful ministry in this church, and gained so much experience that would be very valuable to us in years to come. I also served as interim pastor of Green Memorial Baptist Church in Little Rock, Arkansas; and Woodson Baptist Church in Woodson, Arkansas.

The Lord has blessed our lives and ministry in so many wonderful ways. We can never praise Him enough for who He is and for what He has done. If a person does not know the Lord in a personal way, by being born again, they do not know what life is. Jesus is life.

Chapter 2

My Calling to Childcare Work

When my sister and I went to live with our grandparents, they lived in an old farmhouse that was in need or repair. They were not able to repair the house as it did not belong to them and they did not have the money to do the repairs.

My grandfather was not able to work all the time due to a depressed economy and his poor health. He worked whenever he could. We lived on state assistance whenever he was unable to work.

My grandfather was the type person who would give you the shirt off his back, even though he was not a Christian. He would not have anything to do with the Lord or the church and he would not let my grandmother attend church.

The house we lived in leaked so bad that we had to put containers around to catch the water when it rained. They finally came up with the idea of hanging plastic from the ceiling upstairs, down the walls so that the water would run to one location. Our bathroom was about one hundred feet from the house. In the winter, the snow would blow through the cracks in the door, and we would have to brush it off the seat. This was very exciting when the temperature was thirty degrees below zero or colder. It made for a very memorable experience to say the least. To this day, the bathroom is the one room that I appreciate the most in our home. I have thanked the Lord many, many times for it, especially in the winter. I was almost a teenager before I had taken a bath in a bathtub. Prior to that a bath meant bathing in a No. 3 washtub.

We did not have a car when I was growing up, so wherever we went, we walked unless someone picked us up and gave us a ride. It was seven miles into town where we bought groceries. When we had to buy groceries, we would find someone that we could ride home with.

Our meals were mostly boiled potatoes and vegetables. Meat was a rare treat, except for salt pork strips. Saturday night we always had baked beans and "brown bread". That was always quite a treat. It was also a real treat to have store bought bread once in awhile.

From the time I was in the fourth grade, I would pick potatoes in the fall to earn the money to buy my clothes. Each fall I would buy two pair of wool pants, two shirts, a pair of shoes, long underwear and socks. These would have to last me all school year. One year, I earned enough money picking potatoes to buy a Western Flyer bicycle. I was so proud of that bike.

When I was fifteen I went to live with my mother and step-dad. He wanted me to work in the restaurant they owned. I went to live with them one weekend and started work the next Monday. I went to work at 5:00 in the morning and worked until 10:00 at night. I got paid $2.00 a week. When I received my driver's license, I was permitted to go out on Friday night. When I started work at the restaurant, my step-dad gave me the jobs of the waitress and the dish-washer and let those people go. He cut his overhead expense considerably.

During the school year it was very hard to make passing grades because I was not given any time to study. The teachers understood my predicament and helped any way they could.

When I was seventeen I discovered that I could join the Air Force and take the GED test to get my diploma. I did not want to quit school; however, I did not want to continue in the circumstances I was in either. I did not have time to study and could not take part in athletics or any other school activity.

My mother agreed to sign the papers for me to enlist in the Air Force. I took my GED test and got my diploma, and then starting taking college courses while in the Air Force. I was planning to make the Air Force a career, but the Lord had other plans for me.

Today, experiences like mine and similar experiences take place every day. Thousands of children have to be cared for by someone else. This is what God was calling me to do.

While pastoring Douglasville First Baptist Church, and attending Ouachita Baptist University, I felt the Lord calling me to the childcare ministry. I was commuting to Ouachita in 1963, when the Lord spoke to me concerning this. I knew. He was calling me to start a home for homeless children.

I thought everyone would want to help in such a worthy cause, but what a surprise I was in for. I was soon to learn that not everyone felt the way I did about helping children. Even though people did not feel as I did, I never believed anyone would try to do something to stop me from caring for homeless children, but this was to be my fate.

I have always been the type person who would not deliberately try to hurt anyone, and if I thought I had offended someone, I could not live with it until I corrected it. It always bothered me if I thought someone was upset with me or had something against me. This caused me to be very defensive, which was not good. The Lord has taught me that He is the only one I need to be concerned about pleasing. He would take care of everyone else. Satan can get us too concerned about what people think and greatly affect our effectiveness for God.

Chapter 3

My Previous Callings

I was saved in February, 1960 in Mountain Home, Idaho, while serving in the Air Force. I was planning to make the Air Force my career, however, the Lord called me to preach in March, 1960. I believed at that time it was a special ministry, but did not know the details of it.

I started preaching immediately in the church where I was saved, as well as any other church where I had the opportunity to do so.

There was a new mission started that summer in Boise, Idaho, which is now Calvary Baptist Church. They invited me to preach for them until we left Idaho to go to school at Oachita Baptist University in Arkadelphia, Arkansas. I was their first pastor.

After starting to school in September, 1960 I continued to preach with every opportunity. I was praying if it was God's will for me to be in evangelistic work, however, God closed that door.

I was unable to continue in college because of our finances. Neither my wife nor I could find work in the area where we were attending college. We were without transportation and spent the first part of our college career sleeping on the floor of the apartment the college had provided for us. Our furniture was supposed to be sent to us by the Air Force, but it was lost, as well as the money they owed us when we got out of the Air Force.

When we were ready to leave the military, we were told it would be impossible for us to be discharged that day because of the time involved in processing out of the service, however, the Lord performed some miracles and everything was taken care of between 10:00 A.M. and 5:00 P.M. and that afternoon we were on our way.

After a period of time our furniture and money was located, however, we had to leave school in order to find employment to make enough money to go to school. I started working as a salesman in the insurance business which gave me a good income and gave me the freedom I needed as far as the ministry was concerned.

In 1963 I was able to start back to college I also started pastoring my first church, which was the First Baptist Church of Douglasville, which is a community in southwest little Rock, Arkansas. I know the Lord was not calling me to be a regular Pastor as such, however, I know He was calling me to this particular church to get the experience I needed for the ministry that He had called me to. It was a very difficult church and had many serious problems and they had run off numerous preachers, however, I knew it was God's specific will that I accept the church.

A pastor friend of mine who heard that the church had extended a call to me begged me not to go because of what he though it would do to my ministry, but before the conversation was over, he said if I was certain God was leading me then I had to go. We had a wonderful ministry while there for approximately five years, and could have remained, but we felt the Lord leading us to resign to get the groundwork laid for the special ministry He was calling us to.

While in the church the Lord blessed in many wonderful ways. We saw a large number of people saved, numerous of them who were members of the church already. On one occasion we were in a spirit of revival for six months. God was doing a marvelous work. He completely solved all the problems the church previously had, to the extent that we did not so much as have one sun-in with any of the people who had caused the previous problems. The Lord tripled our attendance and he increased our offering five to seven times what it had been previously and gave us a beautiful new sanctuary. The old sanctuary was remodeled for better educational space and a fellowship hall. This also brought about additional property for parking. It was a very difficult thing when we left the church, for us and the people, because God was blessing in such a marvelous way. During the time I was pastor of this church, I was also attending school and had started my own business from my previous sales experience. With my own business, I was free to come and go as I chose so I was considered fulltime by the church.

After leaving Douglasville, Green memorial Baptist Church in little Rock, Arkansas, extended a call t us to be their fulltime pastor. We shared with them God's calling on our lives and we would be unable to accept the call, but would be willing to fill in for them until they could call a pastor. They then extended a call for us to be the interim pastor and we accepted this call because we felt it was God's will and it wouldn't interfere with what God had already called us to do. We were able to serve this church as a fulltime pastor would and they extended further calls to us to accept it fulltime or be part-time and continue with our other activities. Bet we told them we felt the Lord was only leading us to serve on an interim basis. We were there eight months and had a wonderful ministry. This was also a church with many problems and they had also run off numerous preachers.

After Green memorial Baptist Church called a fulltime pastor we went to Woodson Baptist Church in Woodson, Arkansas to supply and they extended a call for us to accept the church, however we told them the same thing that we could not accept it as regular pastor, but would consider being the interim pastor until they could call someone. God also gave us a beautiful ministry there and they were a wonderful church. We were there eleven months. After being there for numerous months, we began to wonder if maybe the Lord was leading us to become their regular pastor. The church had continued to extend that call to us. After much prayer about it, it was confirmed that we were not to accept the call and shortly thereafter they called a regular pastor.

We have gone back to each of these churches on numerous occasions to preach and still have a wonderful relationship with them.

After leaving Woodson Church, we went back to the Green memorial to be in charge of the outreach Ministry which we did until we moved to Circle H Youth Ranch on a fulltime basis.

In 1971 we heard of property in Dardanelle, Arkansas, that we could purchase to begin our work with homeless children. While speaking to a civic group in that town, I mentioned the available property and a banker in the audience talked with me later saying he would help us get the property, which he did. It was completely undeveloped bit it was a start. In the summer of 1972, the Lord makes another piece of property available, 160 acres which we now have. It was completely developed with a living suite in which we could immediately begin to take children. Three chicken houses that housed 50,000 chickens per growout, which would produce approximately $30,000.00 income per year and approximately 80 head of cattle. The chicken income was used to retire the mortgage. We sold the previous property and made an offer on the 160 acres. Before we could get things closed the lady selling eh property changed her mind and it looked a though we wouldn't get it. This really made it difficult because it appeared the Lord had changed His mind, but we knew this was not the case. My wife and I had prayer claiming the property and the Lord dealt with the lady to the extent that she knew she must sell the property to us. I wrote a check for over $85,000.00 by faith.

We hired a couple in January, 1973 to serve as administrator under our direction. The following summer we moved to the ranch to live fulltime and started having worship services. We have had a lot of difficult times because this type of ministry is an extremely difficult ministry, but also a very rewarding and satisfying ministry. We officially organized our church. Circle H Chapel in 1978 and the following year we stated a Christian school for all 12 grades, using the A.C.E. curriculum. Our church, since being organized, has either been the top church in the top two or three churches in baptisms in our association. We have been the pastor in our present ministry for the past eight years.

I was finally able to get my degree in 1980. I carried a double major in pastoral duties and business administration, so I had considerably more hours than I needed to graduate. I did my last college work in 1974, but did not get around to going through the graduating ceremonies and getting my degree until 1980. The Ministry was just so demanding I could not get it done sooner.

As I mentioned, our church operated a Christian school for all 12 grades. I had been the principal of the school and had also taught in the school. I took the Administrator/Principal training that was required to be a school principal.

I was also involved in counseling in my ministry, no just the normal family counseling and counseling with couples getting married but I also did counseling with children in our care who had many psychological and emotional problem.

We did have a radio ministry for a while. I had been on TV and radio many times, both local and national, sharing our ministry. I was on Dr. D James Kennedy's program twice and on 700 Club numerous times. These were represented on regular network stations.

Chapter 4

Brief History of Our Ministry

We bought property in Perry County, Arkansas, in October, 1972, to start Circle H Youth Ranch. It was first named Circle H Boys Ranch, as we started caring for boys only, then it was not long until we were caring for boys and girls.

I will never forget the first boy who came to Circle H. His name was Tommy W. We were not living at the ranch at this time. We had hired another couple to take care of the children. I was at the ranch the weekend that Tommy came to us, and I will never forget how I felt as I saw him riding across the pasture on one of the horses. I took my daughter, Lisa on my knee and pointed to Tommy, telling her that was what Circle H was all about. There were many children in the world who did not have a mommy and daddy as she did to take care of them. If we had never helped another child, and we did, about two hundred, the feeling of fulfillment and excitement I felt at that time, would have lasted a lifetime. We were to feel this excitement many times over the years of our ministry, but that first boy was something special.

After about eighteen months, my family and I moved to the ranch, which was to be the greatest step of faith we had ever taken. We sold our home and property in Little Rock to move to Perry County. There were many things the Lord had to do so that we could make the move. We had to sell our property, which was done without ever listing it. We had to sell one vehicle and have work done on the other one. The Lord provided all the work and provided a home for us at the ranch. The other houses at the ranch were already filled with children and house parents. There was not enough funds in the ministry for us to receive a salary, so the Lord had to make a way for all our debts to be paid, and a small income from another source. He did all of this and so much more.

We had a business in Little Rock which we left to others, so we had no income from this. We thought that in the future it might provide some income; however, this was not the way the Lord would have it be. We were to have nothing to do with any business, but depend upon God to meet our needs. All we had materially was to be put into the ministry. The ministry was to be our only concern and occupy our total time and effort. It has been the most wonderful experience we have ever had.

People have always been good to our ministry and helped us in many ways. We did not know of anyone who was against the ministry. The local people and the media were very kind to us.

The Childcare Ministry is a very trying ministry in many ways. The children, of course, have many needs and this is very demanding in itself. It is also very hard to get house parents and keep them. They burn out very fast. I always wondered why it was so difficult until the Lord revealed to me that Satan would do everything he could to make it difficult, because he did not want ministries in existence that were dedicated to caring for children. Jesus had much to say about children, especially in Matthew 19:14 "But Jesus said, suffer little children, and forbid them not to come unto me: for of such is the kingdom of heaven." There are numerous scriptures referring to how God feels about children.

Our ministry prospered and grew until we were able to care for thirty or more children. After being in operation for sometime, we were told by Social Services, that a childcare facility must be licensed. We did not understand the consequences of licensing at the time, and did not understand what the Bible taught on the subject. We were told that Social Services wanted to help, and they needed a place for children. Up to that time most of the children we cared for came through Social Services. We had a good relationship with Social Services, and the people in the Perry County office were always very kind and helpful. Their philosophy was totally different from what the basic philosophy is today. However, I might hasten to say, the people in Social Services who really care about children, do not share the new philosophy. More will be said about this in a later chapter.

As our ministry progressed, we realized that these children needed more than love, a home, food and clothing. One of the greatest needs was educational. The vast majority of the children we cared for were years behind academically. They were failing in public school, and most of them could barely read and write, if at all. We accepted a license, thinking there was no other way, and we were willing to accept any help we could get. We did not want to do anything illegal. We did not understand the relationship problem. Many of the children were old enough, that legally they could not be made to go to school. They were continual problems in the local public schools and were not being helped. We knew something had to be done.

After much concern and prayer about their educational needs, the Lord opened the door for me to learn about Accelerated Christian Education. When I saw this Christian School Program, I had a revival in my heart and knew this was the answer to our prayers, and that somehow God would provide the way for us to have a Christian School. He did just that and our church, Circle H Chapel, started Circle H Academy. Our church was not in existence when the childcare ministry first began. We would not accept a license or accreditation on our school. By this time, the Lord was beginning to teach us about licensing.

We were amazed at the progress the children were making in school, and they were excited about this learning experience. It was no problem getting them to go to school, and absenteeism was practically nonexistent. They would have to be really sick not to go. School had become an exciting and rewarding experience. The children felt good about themselves, and began to experience some self-esteem.

The public school had nothing but good things to say about our school. They were helpful and did not hinder what we were doing in any way. The State Education Department visited our school and were very impressed with what we were accomplishing, as you can see in the letter that follows this chapter.

After we accepted a license, we began to experience some harassment by the Licensing Worker from Social Services. She continued to make an issue of the fact we were a Christian facility, and that the children had to learn scripture.

When we started the Christian School, the worker really began to give us a difficult time. Even though our records proved that the children were doing well and learning, and that the State Education Department commended our school, the worker still would not leave us alone.

The State of Arkansas does not require licensing or accreditation of private schools, and in fact, does not have criteria developed for doing so. They have traditionally chosen not to govern private schools. In spite of this, the Licensing Worker still insisted that we must be accredited or the children would not get a good education. On one occasion, I asked her what was most important, that the children go to an accredited school and not receive an education, or go to a non accredited school but get an education. She said that was not the issue. The most important thing was that the school be accredited. I could not conceive of anyone having that type of attitude.

On one occasion, the worker turned in a report stating that we only had two textbooks and one outdated set of encyclopedias in our school. There is no such thing as an outdated set of encyclopedias. They contain history and facts concerning various subjects, things that never change, you just add a yearbook each year to bring it current. At that time, we had all the text material to teach all the children in our care. As a matter of fact, we had an entire wall of bookshelves, filled with books for our school. We also had eight sets of encyclopedias. The worker considered textbooks to be only "hardback" books used by the public school system. There were many false reports given concerning our ministry.

Through all the problems we had with the state, the Lord began to teach us why it was wrong to be licensed.

State of Arkansas
DEPARTMENT OF EDUCATION

STATE EDUCATION BUILDING   LITTLE ROCK, ARKANSAS 72201

STATE BOARD OF EDUCATION
WAYNE HARTSFIELD, Searcy, Chairman
MRS. JAMES W. CHESNUTT, Hot Springs, V. Chairman
T. C. COGBILL, JR., Star City
JIM DuPREE, Weldon
HARRY A. HAINES, Blytheville
DR. HARRY P. McDONALD, Fort Smith
ROBERT L. NEWTON, Warren
MRS. ALICE L. PRESTON, Murfreesboro
WALTER TURNBOW, Springdale

DON R. ROBERTS
    Director

TELEPHONE
371-1461

June 23, 1980

Rev. Don Grendell, Administrator
Circle H Youth Ranch
Star Route, Box 78
Plainview, AR 72857

Dear Rev. Grendell:

The courtesies extended Mr. Benton and me on our recent visit to your ranch by you and others of your staff are appreciated very much.

To say the least, we were impressed with the task you and your organization has undertaken. Clearly, your program is unique to Arkansas.

As mentioned in our conference, it would be unfair to your organization to attempt to meet minimum standards for accrediting elementary schools in Arkansas at the present time. The current policies and regulations were not designed to meet the needs of an organization like yours.

Presently, we are in the process of developing policies and regulations that would better serve organizations like yours. You can help us help you by sending a letter explaining the purpose of your organization, clientele, religious affiliation, curriculum, and other information you deem necessary to Dr. Sherman Peterson, Associate Director for Instructional Services. This letter should also express your stated desire to meet minimum standards for accreditation.

Again, thanks for the courtesies extended on our recent visit. If we can assist you further, please call.

                Sincerely,

                Larry S. Robertson
                Educational Administrative Supervisor

LSR/mw
cc: Mr. Joseph Foster, Jr.
    Mr. E. E. Benton
    Dr. Sherman Peterson
    Child Facility Review Board

"AN EQUAL OPPORTUNITY EMPLOYER"

Chapter 5

Our Stand on Licensing

The reason I feel it is wrong to be licensed is the relationship. Only a greater can license a lesser, and to permit the state to license my ministry, is to place the state over the church. Jesus is the head of the church. To accept a license is to deny God's control over the church.

The ministry of the Lord Jesus is a command of God, as mentioned in Matthew 28:19,20 which states, *"Go ye therefore and teach all nations, baptizing them in the name of the Father, and of the Son, and of the Holy Ghost: Teaching them to observe all things whatsoever I have commanded you, and lo I am with you always, even unto the end of the world"*. The church has a mandate from God to carry out His mission and purpose. Since I have been called personally by the Lord into the ministry, I have a personal mandate to carry out the Great Commission by the calling God has placed on my life, which involves caring for, educating and training children in the Christian faith.

The main purpose of our ministry is to bring children to a saving faith in the Lord Jesus Christ, making total commitment of their lives to God, so they will become the preachers, missionaries, Christian business and professional people of the future. The main objective is the child's salvation, as pointed out in Mark 10:14, *"But when Jesus saw it, he was much displeased, and said unto them, Suffer the little children to come unto me, and forbid them not: for of such is the kingdom of God"*. Our obligation to train the child is given in Ephesians 6:4, *"And, ye fathers, provoke not your children to wrath: but bring them up in the nurture and admonition of the Lord."* Ecclesiastes 12:1, *"Remember now thy Creator in the days of thy youth, while the evil days come not, nor the years draw nigh, when thou shalt say, I have no pleasure in them."* Proverbs 22:6, *"Train up a child in the way he should go: and when he is old, he will not depart from it."*

Children cannot be left to themselves. We believe that we must teach the child to have a God fearing world view. We do not believe in a secular world and a religious world. We believe that all is religious, as is pointed out in 1Cor. 10:31, *"Whether therefore ye eat, or drink, or whatsoever ye do, do all to the glory of God."* 1 Timothy 3:15, *"But if I tarry long, that thou mayest know how thou oughtest to behave thyself in the house of God, which is the church of the living God, the pillar and ground of the truth."* Psalms 14:1, *"The fool hath said in his heart, there is no God. They are corrupt, they have done abominable works, there is none that doeth good."* Psalms 146:7, *"Which executeth judgment for the oppressed: which giveth food to the hungry. The Lord looseth the prisoners."*

We believe in the total stewardship of life, not only our time, talents and money, but our entire body and mind belong to the Lord Jesus Christ, as we were bought and paid for at Calvary, as it is pointed out in Acts 20:24, *"But none of these things move me, neither count I my life dear unto myself, so that I might finish my course with joy, and the ministry, which I have received of the Lord Jesus, to testify the gospel of the grace of God."* 1 Corinthians 6:20, *"For ye are bought with a price: therefore glorify God in your body and in your spirit, which are God's."* 1 Corinthians 7:23, *"Ye are bought with a price, be not yet the servants of men".* We are not free to act as we want, because we belong to Christ lock, stock and barrel.

We believe that Jesus is Lord over the church as Paul points out in Ephesians 1:22, *"And hath put all things under His feet, and gave Him to be the head over all things to the church".* He is Sovereign and is the Head, no one can take His place.

Licensure represents control, as only a greater can license a lesser. The state should not dictate the policies of the church. Colossians 1:18, *"And he is the head of the body, the church: who is the beginning, the first born from the dead; that in all things He might have the preeminence".*

Licensure does not insure quality, as it is said that Jim Jones had at least six licenses, and received many thousands of dollars in federal funds. I personally feel that licensure tends to create problems in religious ministries, because when we are licensed, people tend to believe it is quality and therefore, a lot of wrong things can be done as a result of it. The problems are not controlled.

God ordained three institutions. The home, the church and the government, and each has its function to perform. Society functions best when all three institutions do their part as given them by God; however, problems arise when one institution assumes the responsibility of one of the others. The function of government according to Romans 13:1-14 is, *"Let every soul be subject unto the higher powers that are ordained of God: and they that resist shall receive to themselves damnation. For rulers are not a terror to good works, but to the evil. Wilt thou then not be afraid of the power? Do that which is good, and thou shalt have praise of the same: For he is the minister of God to thee for good. But if thou do that which is evil, be afraid; for he beareth not the sword in vain: for he is the minister of God, a revenger to execute wrath upon him that doeth evil. Wherefore, ye must needs be subject, not only for wrath, but also for conscience sake. For this cause pay ye tribute also: for they are God's ministers, attending continually upon this very thing. Render therefore to all their dues: tribute to whom tribute is due, custom to whom custom; fear to whom fear, honor to whom honor. Owe no man anything, but to love one another: for he that loveth another hath fulfilled the law. For this, thou shalt not commit adultery. Thou shalt not kill, thou shalt not steal, thou shalt not bear false witness, thou shalt not covet; and if there be any other commandment, it is briefly comprehended in this saying, namely, thou shalt love thy neighbor as thyself. Love worketh no ill to his neighbor: therefore love is the fulfilling of the law. And that, knowing the time, that now it is high time to awake out of sleep: for now is our salvation nearer than when we believed. The night is far spent, the day is at hand, let us therefore cast off the works of darkness, and let us put on the armor of light. Let us walk honestly, as in the day; not in rioting and drunkenness, not in wantonness, not in strife and envying. But put ye on the Lord Jesus Christ and make not provision for the flesh, to fulfill the lusts therefore."* The function of the government is to reward good and punish evil. We as Christians recognize the fact that government should be concerned with three areas pertaining to our ministry, which are fire, health and safety. We have no problem with that because it is ordained of God. The problem arises when government gets out of its role given them by God, and begins to involve itself in the role of the church, as is happening today.

As Christians, we are law abiding citizens; however, when the laws of men are contrary to the laws of God, then we find ourselves in the position that Peter, John and others found themselves in Acts 4:19,20, *"But Peter and John answered and said unto them, whether it be right in the sight of God to hearken unto you more than unto God, judge ye. For we cannot but speak the things which we have seen and heard."*

You do not find the rapes, murders and property damage in our Christian Schools that you find in the public schools. You will also find that children graduating from Christian Schools obtain a better education, and are better equipped for college and life in general. Children in Christian Schools are not disrespectful, disobedient or poorly groomed.

Standards are not the problem, as the standards we impose on ourselves are higher than those imposed by a government agency. The problem with licensure is relationship.

Chapter 6

The Attack

The first part of 1982, the Lord convicted me of the sin I had committed by accepting a license on the Children's Home part of our ministry. I asked God to forgive me and began taking steps to correct the problem.

There was a law on the books in Arkansas allowing for religious exemption from licensing of childcare facilities. However, it allowed this for only those facilities started prior to July, 1969. This did not appear to be a problem since our ministry started prior to this, and we received our nonprofit status in 1968. It seemed to me that we should have no problem. I found that the State Social Services had no intention of permitting religious exemption. They said we were not a childcare facility until they declared us to be one, and that wasn't until 1974, when we accepted a license.

Prior to telling the state we could no longer accept a license, we had been referred to as one of the largest and best childcare facilities in the state. They would bring people out to tour our facilities. Once we informed them we could no longer be licensed and asked for exemption, they began their attack. All of a sudden, we began to be referred to as lawbreakers, child abusers and a nuisance to our community. Isn't it strange that we became so bad overnight. Isn't it strange that license assures quality and legality, and lack of license means you are illegal and lack quality. It is amazing what a little piece of paper can do for a person. What awesome power!

When we met with the Childcare Licensing Review Board concerning religious exemption, we met with quite a surprise. The attorney for Social Services introduced child abuse charges against us and said that the children in our care were in "imminent danger". This seemed strange as prior to our refusal to accept a license, we received calls daily from Social Services asking us to take children.

The abuse charges they brought up were allegations made by some former children the year before. The allegations had been investigated by Social Services and were found to be non-substantiated. Social Services policy states that if there are allegations against a childcare facility, the allegations are to be investigated and if non-substantiated they will be expunged from the record in ninety days. The County Office did this, but the State Office did not. They keep a file of these allegations to use against Christian Childcare facilities. They have gone back twenty years in some cases. The County Social Services Office told the state attorney that there was no truth to the allegations but that did not make any difference.

In a few days, a lawsuit was filed with all those allegations, plus many more. It was amended many times to add new allegations. The media picked up on it and really sensationalized it, which is exactly what Social Services wanted. In my opinion, this was done to sway the public. I contacted a State Representative about it and he contacted the Commissioner of Social Services. He told the Commissioner it was wrong to use the media the way they were, and he knew the allegations were false. The Commissioner told him the lawsuit would be dropped if we would take a license. Isn't it strange that they would license a facility they believed to be as terrible as they said ours was. The contact by the State Representative did no good, the attack continued. The following is a copy of the lawsuit, so you can see how ridiculous their allegations were.

In addition to the charges in the lawsuit, an assistant Attorney General, called my wife and I "Mr. and Mrs. Hitler". He also said on a Little Rock radio station, that I "beat the children with a whip". They had a special State Police Investigator visit with twenty of the former children we cared for to try to prove abuse. The children stated they received paddling when they needed it, but they did not say they were ever abused. In fact, some of the children said the licks they got were not excessive, and they did not get all they really deserved. When the report went to the state, they announced that all twenty children were abused. There was continual harassment and degrading articles in the newspapers. The media shared the same philosophy that the state had. It is impossible to get both sides of the story printed. The media, for the most part, is very credential oriented; therefore they believe that the only way any program can have quality is to be licensed.

In my opinion, licensing does not assure quality. On the contrary, it tends to promote just the opposite. Anyone can get a license and when they do, everyone assumes they are legitimate. If that is the case, then Jim Jones must have been top quality, because I understand he had six licenses. Now, I think the average individual is smart enough to know that he wasn't.

When you have a license, there is an annual visit by a so-called "Licensing Specialist". Are people so deceived as to believe that a visit once a year is going to assure that no wrong is taking place. Is it going to protect the children from abuse? Certainly not! It is absurd to insult the intelligence of an individual by trying to convince him that it will.

People have admitted that they make the necessary changes to meet the standards of licensing when notification of a licensing visit is received. They have additional staff members present, they do various things at the time which they do not do the remainder of the year. Who is fooling who? Whenever there is a child abuse allegation made against a licensed facility, the allegation is checked out and if not substantiated, it is dropped. That is as it should be; however, if it is substantiated, the child is removed and the person who is guilty is dealt with, and sometimes not severely enough. They tend to play it down because the facility is licensed. But, let an abuse allegation be made against a Christian non-licensed facility, and a lawsuit will follow by Social Services, even though it is non-substantiated. It will also be all over the news. It is played up instead of down, and it is sensationalized. You might ask why this is true. It is very simple. It is a matter of control. The state wants to control all the facilities, and it has nothing to do with quality or protection for the children.

If a person will check the facts, I think they will find there are more abuse incidents in licensed childcare facilities than in the Christian non-licensed facilities.

If there was no relationship problem with licensing of Christian ministries, it would still be impossible to accept a license because of the state's philosophy, they say you can't paddle a child at all, even though it is done as a last resort, and the Bible teaches that we are to do it. Who are they to override the Word of God?

They also say that you can't make the children attend church, even though it is known you are a Christian ministry, and that is one of the requirements. The parents, or whoever placed the child is in agreement with the requirement, and in fact, that is one of the reasons the child is placed with you. The state says that the desire of the child overrides the desire of the parent. In other words, the child's right supersedes the parents rights. Do you realize how unscriptural this is? That idea was born in the pits of hell.

It is one of the main philosophies of ACLU and all humanists. The state says a child will be hindered in getting a higher education if he attends a Christian School that is not accredited. This, of course, is another lie. They know that no college can refuse them. Let's stop kidding ourselves and look at the facts. The results will be amazing.

Children who attend A.C.E. Schools consistently test in the top ten percent of all children tested. The largest single group of children in Christian Schools are the children of public school teachers and administrators, because they know the quality of education the child receives. On the average, the children in A.C.E. Schools are two grade levels above the public school. When these children graduate, they have the equivalent of the first year of college behind them and can test out of their first year of college. I could go on and on with the facts about these schools, but I think what I have said makes the point.

When we were in court, we never had the privilege of showing the children's school records, so that the facts might speak for themselves. The state does not want to consider the actual facts. They do not want to test the children in public school and compare these tests with the tests of children in Christian Schools, because they know what the results would be. Results are not the issue, nor is a good education the issue. Control is the issue. You will find that most of the educators in the public school system are very humanistic and credential oriented. Our educational system has gone down the drain. Our government has admitted this in a report they did on public education called "A Nation At Risk". If you have not read it, you should do so. It will be an eye-opening experience and one that will probably scare you to death.

It is my understanding that ACLU has vowed to close down every Christian childcare facility in the country. They said they would rather see the children on the streets in prostitution and on drugs than in Christianity. Nice folks, aren't they. Their name, American Civil Liberties Union sounds very American. As American as "apple pie" as the saying goes. But this is the way Satan works. He whitewashes everything. He makes the counterfeit look very real. The sad thing is, most Christians fall for it.

I could go on and on about all the lies that were propagated about our ministry, such as the property being guarded with loaded weapons and many more bizarre and ridiculous things. However, I do not think belaboring the point will help any. I think I have said enough that any open-minded and concerned Christian can see, there are some very serious problems in our country. I hope that you will be stirred enough to take a stand for what is right.

IN THE CHANCERY COURT OF PERRY COUNTY, ARKANSAS

ARKANSAS SOCIAL SERVICES   PLAINTIFF

VS.   NO. E-82-52

CIRCLE H YOUTH RANCH,
AN ARKANSAS NOT FOR PROFIT
CORPORATION   DEFENDANT

TEMPORARY RESTRAINING ORDER

Now on this 14th day of July, 1982 the above matter proceeds on to a hearing pursuant to Rule 65 of the Arkansas Rules of Civil Procedure and Ark. Stat. Ann. §83-915 and upon the Complaint and Request for Temporary Restraining Order and Injunction of the Plaintiff.

The Court being well and sufficiently advised as to all matters of law and fact before it makes the following findings:

(1) Circle H Youth Ranch is an Arkansas non-profit corporation doing business in Perry County, Arkansas as a residential youth facility in violation of Ark. Stat. Ann. §83-903 in that it is unlicensed by the Arkansas Child Care Facility Review Board.

(2) The Court has jurisdiction of this matter pursuant to Ark. Stat. Ann. §83-915.

(3) Plaintiff has demonstrated the likelihood of success on the merits of its Complaint and the imminent danger of irreparable harm to the approximately 16 juveniles being housed in this unlicensed facility.

(4) Defendant and its officers, agents, representatives, and employees should be and are hereby immediately enjoined, restrained and prohibited from operating said facility and from housing said juveniles at the facility pending a hearing and further orders of this Court.

IT IS THEREFORE ORDERED, ADJUDGED AND DECREED that Circle H Youth Ranch and its officers, agents, representatives, and employees are immediately enjoined, prohibited and restrained from operating as a child care facility and from housing juveniles at said factility pending a hearing and further orders of this Court.

CHANCELLOR, PERRY COUNTY
CHANCERY COURT

DATE: 7/14/82

FILED

IN THE CHANCERY COURT OF PERRY COUNTY, ARKANSAS

ARKANSAS SOCIAL SERVICES   PLAINTIFF

VS.   NO. E-82-52

CIRCLE H YOUTH RANCH,
AN ARKANSAS NOT FOR PROFIT
CORPORATION AND DON GRENDELL,
EXECUTIVE DIRECTOR   DEFENDANTS

AMENDED COMPLAINT AND REQUEST FOR
TEMPORARY AND PERMANENT INJUNCTION

Comes now the Plaintiff, by and through its attorneys, Steve Clark, Attorney General, Robert L. Waldrum, Assistant Attorney General and Judieth Balentine, Social Services Attorney and for its Amendment to the Complaint originally filed in this action, state and allege as follows as a second cause of action:

1. Plaintiff amends the Complaint to join Mr. Don Grendell, Executive Director of Circle H Youth Ranch, and a resident of Perry County, Arkansas as a party defendant.

2. Mr. Grendell is Director of Defendant Ranch and as such is legally responsible for the total operation of the Ranch, the actions of its personnel, those currently employed and employed since 1974 when Circle H was originally licensed by the Child Care Facility Review Board.

3. Mr. Grendell has been the Ranch's Director since 1974 until the current time and was directly aware of and responsible for the mistreatment, physical and emotional, and/or unlawful jailing of numerous juveniles, while under his supervision, in the Perry County jail.

4. From 1974 until the current date, Mr. Grendell has

4. From 1974 until the current date, Mr. Grendell has implemented an ongoing policy of abusive whippings of the juvenile residents at the Ranch with belts, leather straps and wooden objects.

5. During this time, Mr. Grendell ordered that metal bars be placed on all windows of the Ranch cottages in addition to padlocks on the doors.

6. Mr. Grendell and Circle H Ranch have no legal authority to imprison juveniles in this manner.

7. Mr. Grendell and Circle H Ranch have no legal authority to physically confine juveniles against their will at the Ranch.

8. Mr. Grendell has assisted in unlawfully imprisoning juveniles residing at his facility in the Perry County jail without any criminal charge or other lawful justification for the jailings as listed in attached Exhibit A.

9. Mr. Grendell and/or his employees have called the Perry County Sheriff's deputies to remove and/or jail juveniles at the Ranch for no criminal charge or other lawful justification as listed in Exhibit A.

10. It is a violation of the juveniles' rights under the Fifth and Fourteenth Amendments of the Constitution of the United States, for any person to cause or actively assist in causing their imprisonment, without a criminal charge, in an adult detention facility.

11. Mr. Grendell and employees of the Circle H Ranch have caused and/or assisted in causing the jailings of the juveniles listed in Exhibit A without lawfully bringing any criminal charges or other lawful justification for such jailings.

12. Mr. Grendell and/or Circle H employees summoned a Perry County deputy sheriff to remove Dewayne Harper from Circle H Ranch and jail him in the Perry County jail on

June 28, 1981 without any criminal charge.

13. This jailing of Dewayne Harper was instigated by Mr. Grendell or Ranch personnel for Harper's refusal to attend church services at the Ranch.

14. Circle H and Mr. Grendell have enforced in the past and are enforcing now a policy of punishing juveniles at the Ranch for not attending religious services either by whippings or causing the juveniles to lose merit points in the Ranch's merit-demerit point system.

15. The policy of compelling religious attendance is a violation of the juveniles legal rights under the First and Fourteenth Amendments to the United States Constitution.

16. Mr. Grendell and/or Circle H employees locked Dottie [Doe] alone in her room at the Ranch for one week as punishment for some infraction of the Ranch's rules.

17. Other juveniles at the Ranch have been similarly locked in their rooms.

18. Such practice is emotionally abusive to the juveniles.

19. More than a dozen juvenile residents have run away from the Ranch because of abusive treatment, whippings and mistreatment including but not limited to the juveniles named in Exhibit A.

20. Currently and in the past Circle H has housed mentally retarded juveniles and has failed to provide the special education mandated under Public Law 94-142.

21. These mentally retarded juveniles have been whipped by Mr. Grendell and his staff with belts, leather straps or wooden objects.

22. A specific mentally retarded child named Harold [Doe] currently at the Ranch has been whipped many times including once when he received 25 licks from Ranch employee Pete Griffin for bed wettings.

23. A specific juvenile at the Ranch now has a speech impediment which is so severe that he cannot speak intelligibly and yet he receives no speech therapy at the Ranch for this condition.

24. A juvenile named Ray [Doe], who has left the Ranch, was punished by being forced to wear only a towel as his only clothing for a week and had to work in the fields at the Ranch with only this towel.

25. Such punishment is emotionally and physically abusive.

26. Mr. Grendell and/or the staff at Circle H have enforced a policy of opening, reading and destroying mail coming to its residents or leaving the Ranch from its residents.

27. Mr. Grendell and Circle H staff enforce a policy of withholding food from the juveniles as punishment.

28. Juveniles at the Ranch are whipped so often that no written records of such corporal punishment are maintained by the Ranch staff or Mr. Grendell.

29. The "school" at Circle H Ranch is not accredited by any governmental agency, nor are the juveniles at Circle H allowed to attend a governmentally accredited school, thus damaging any future opportunity at an institution of higher learning.

30. Currently and in the past the Ranch and Mr. Grendell have neglected the nutritional needs of the juveniles by withholding food as punishment and serving meals which do not meet even the minimum needs of these children.

31. In view of the foregoing it is clear that Circle H Ranch and its Director are a public nuisance and a threat to the health, safety and welfare of the juveniles it recruits and abuses.

JURISDICTION

32. In addition to the statutory jurisdiction which Plaintiff seeks to invoke pursuant to Ark. Stat. Ann. §83-915 (Repl. 1976) in the original Complaint (first cause of action), Plaintiff herein invokes the common law jurisdiction of the court of equity as an alternative and independently separate cause of action, to abate a public nuisance. Ozark Poultry Products, Inc. v. Garman, 251 Ark. 389, 472 S.W.2nd 714.

33. The acts complained of herein all occurred in Perry County, Arkansas thus establishing jurisdiction in the Perry County Chancery Court.

34. Circle H Ranch and Mr. Grendell, while a private non-profit corporation and its Executive Director respectively, hold themselves out to the public as a place where parents, courts, or governmental agencies may send children for care, education, room and board at the cost of approximately $200.00 a month.

35. Defendants actively advertise and encourage the public to send their children there.

36. Once there the children are physically and emotionally abused, whipped, threatened, jailed, and have numerous Constitutional rights abused and abridged.

37. This mistreatment of juveniles is an established pattern since 1974 and will continue unless enjoined.

38. Arkansas Social Services has standing to bring this action as the state agency with legislative authority to protect and safeguard the state's children.

39. The damage and harm complained of herein is indeed irreparable in that emotional and physical abuse to children leaves scars that will last a lifetime.

WHEREFORE, Premises Considered, Plaintiff alternatively prays for an injunction against Defendants to restrain and prohibit them from operating a youth care facility and/or housing any juveniles.

VERIFICATION

STATE OF ARKANSAS)
)ss
COUNTY OF PULASKI)

I, Robert L. Waldrum, Assistant Attorney General, hereby state under oath that the facts set forth in the foregoing Amended Complaint and Request for Temporary and Permanent Injunction are true and correct to the best of my knowledge, information and belief.

ROBERT L. WALDRUM

Subscribed and sworn to before me, a Notary Public, on this 5th day of July, 1982.

NOTARY PUBLIC

My Commission Expires:
August 16, 1989

ARKANSAS SOCIAL SERVICES

STEVE CLARK
Attorney General

BY: _____
ROBERT L. WALDRUM
Assistant Attorney General
Justice Building
Little Rock, Arkansas 72201

AND

_____
JUDIETH BALENTINE
Attorney for Arkansas Social
   Services
1031 Donaghey Building
Little Rock, Arkansas 72201

CERTIFICATE OF SERVICE

I, Robert L. Waldrum, Assistant Attorney General, do hereby certify that a copy of the foregoing Amended Complaint and Request for Temporary and Permanent Injunction has been served by U.S. Mail, postage prepaid, this __15__ day of July, 1982 to Mr. James Marschewski, Attorney at Law, P.O. Box 1004, Russellville, Arkansas 72801; Mr. Peter Miller, Attorney at Law, 955 Tower Building, Little Rock, Arkansas 72201 and Mr. Richard Moore, Attorney at Law, Gibbs and Craze, 6929 West 130th, Room 600, Cleveland, Ohio 44130.

_____
ROBERT L. WALDRUM

Chapter 7

The Outcome

By now, you are probably wondering what happened to our ministry. You might say, "surely, all those lies were not believed". You are partially correct. The general public did not seem to believe it, as we received calls and letters from all over the country saying the people were praying for us, and they knew what we were doing was of the Lord.

This was very encouraging. When people sent donations to help in our battle, we were very touched and praised the Lord for the prayers and financial support. We learned to trust the Lord to greater depths through our experience. The peace and victory we experienced was wonderful and there is no way that it can be expressed in words. I really believed that people would stand with us to the extent that all the funds needed to fight the enemy would be provided. However, I learned that this was another area that I was very naive in. People just do not realize how expensive an attack like this is. It cost us approximately $100,000.00 in expense and loss of income. When you consider that our total budget for the year was only $120,000.00, you can see how impossible it was for us to continue financially.

During the course of the lawsuit, the state attorneys told our attorney that it didn't matter how the lawsuit came out, "they were going to get Don Grendell". They said they would file criminal charges against me, or do whatever they had to put me out of business. One must understand, they have an unlimited source of funds to work with, our tax dollars.

So many people are prone to say "it is not my battle", so they do not help in any way, not realizing it is their battle, because it is not an individual they are attacking, but the church. If you are part of the church, the body of Christ, then the attack is against you also. It is just a matter of time until you will feel it directly. Things are going to get progressively worse unless Christians are willing to stand together, regardless of denomination. Don't misunderstand me, I am not promoting the World Council of Churches, or an ecumenical movement. What I am talking about is born again, Bible believing, fundamental, conservative Christians, who stand together, regardless of their doctrinal differences. There is just one enemy and that is Satan, not some other church.

When we had the preliminary hearing, things looked rather positive, because the judge seemed to be understanding. At the beginning he said he did not necessarily consider giving a child licks with a paddle to be abusive. There were other things that gave us hope, such as another statement made by the judge, stating it was evident that the state attorneys had coached their witnesses. He also said he did not think the public school was the best place for every child.

During the course of the hearings, two Social Services employees from our county, testified in our behalf, acknowledging that the allegations were false. As a matter of fact, they told the state attorney the allegations were false before we went to court; however, that did not change the state's plan. You can see that the facts were not important.

As a result of the testimony given by one of the County Social Services workers, she experienced harassment and would have lost her job had it not been for political intervention. They made terrible accusations against her while they had her on the witness stand, knowing there was no truth to any of them. The state was willing to turn on their own people in order to satisfy their goals.

The state was rather surprised when they found that the children would not lie on the witness stand as they thought they would. As a matter of fact, the state was so surprised, they only used a few of the children they had brought in to testify. The children they did use, did not help their case, and some refused to say the things the state wanted them to say.

One of the most surprising things to the state was when they brought the children in, they came running to me, my wife and other staff members, saying they didn't know why they had to be there. They said the state attorneys told them they had no choice. When it came time to go to lunch, the children were told they had to go to lunch with the state worker who had brought them to court. Some of the children refused to go and said they were going to lunch with the people from Circle H. What a blow this was to the state.

The following is a copy of the Court Order given at the end of the hearing. I might add though, that we were not given the right to put all our witnesses on the stand, nor did we have opportunity to put on evidence concerning our school. The Judge said he had heard enough, which led us to believe he would rule in our favor. The state had a day and a half to put on their testimony and we had half a day. You can see from this, Christians are not given their constitutional rights in court.

When we went to court, we did not have the right to go before a regular judge. A special judge was appointed. The regular judges did not want to touch it. The special judge was selected by the attorneys who were in the courthouse at the time the hearing was set. Guess who they were? Not ours!

I was told if I ever violated the contempt order that was placed on me, it would be enforced. It has never been dropped. I was also told that if I was ever in court again concerning my ministry, we would not be able to go before a regular judge, but would have to go before the same person who was appointed for the hearings. The special judge stated that if I was back in court again, he would probably rule against us. There is nothing like a decision being made before the facts are presented. However, that seems to be the way the original hearing was, the results were known before the hearing took place. What has happened to our constitutional rights as Christians.

As you can see from the Court Order, the state was unable to prove their case; however, the Judge still ordered our ministry to cease, based on the testimony of the Commissioner of Social Services. She said she had evaluated our school and found it 'woefully inadequate'. This was untrue. She had been to our facility one time during the summer the year before. While there, she was in the school less than thirty minutes. I think it would take more than a miracle to accomplish what she testified to.

I later talked to one of the state people who had visited the facility with her and asked him, if in his opinion she did an evaluation of the school. His answer was "no".

Before the hearings began, our attorneys offered a motion for the lawsuit to be dropped as we only had six children at that time. We said that we would keep no more than this until the issue was resolved legislatively. The law in Arkansas allows a facility to have up to six children without a license. We were denied this right.

The Judge admitted that we had not violated the law; however, he said we could, so he would go on with the hearing.

After the hearings, the state attorney agreed with our attorneys that we could call the parents who had placed the children in our facility, so they could pick them up and return them home. I did this and almost immediately received a call from the Judge saying that he was considering a contempt order against me for moving the children. The state attorney evidently called the Judge and told him we were moving the children, denying that she had agreed to this. They did not have a contempt hearing at this time.

Our ministry had to continue because God called me to it, not the state. I could not disobey God. I told the Judge in court, if I was ordered to stop my ministry, I would have to continue. I also pointed out what it would do to us financially if he ordered me to cease my ministry. None of this made any difference.

There was a child who was eighteen and could not be considered; therefore, he remained with us and because of this, our ministry continued. We wanted to obey the court order as long as it didn't mean disobeying God's commands. God's law and His Word must always supersede all other laws.

Some months after we were ordered to close, we made another request of the court to have the six children that the law allowed. On this occasion the request was granted. I do not know why this was not approved at the start of the hearings to save all the time and money. Even though the request was granted, it was not done until the Judge first held me in contempt of court for continuing my ministry. Isn't that ironic? We were only doing what God called us to do and what the law allowed, yet I was held in contempt of court, and then permitted to do it.

When I was held in contempt of court, the state wanted me put in jail; however, the Judge would not do this. In lieu of that, they wanted him to fine me $5,000, knowing that I could not pay it and would have to go to jail, so the end result would be the same. The Judge didn't do that either. He settled on a fine of $1,000, but immediately suspended it.

Even though we had the right to continue our ministry, and was authorized by the court to do so, the state was not content. They tried to bring further action against me.

On one occasion to fulfill their threat to file criminal charges against me, they sent another State Police investigator to see me in an effort to prove that I was taking money from the children and putting it in my account. This of course got nowhere, but they were determined to continue their harassment in order to ruin me in anyway they could.

On another occasion, they filed a lawsuit against the parents of a child who had formerly been with us, adding my name in the paperwork and calling me a defendant to the lawsuit. Of course, I wasn't. However, they were going to try to hold me in contempt of court through it. I was notified about two and a half hours before I was to be in court in another county. I did not have time to get legal counsel or answer the allegations. You normally have twenty days to do this. They were unable to do anything to me, other than cause further harassment. They continued to circulate rumors about me and my ministry, even though our childcare facility, our school and church was closed, because we were unable to continue financially.

On one occasion, a newspaper reporter called trying to get some information in order to write a story to defame our ministry. I was gone at the time and Mary told the reporter he would have to call back and talk to me. He asked who she was, not knowing she was my wife. He was apparently going to try to twist her words around and still do his "dirty work". When she would not give her name or any information, he later called back and disguised his voice. When she answered the phone, he asked who he was talking to, and she told him before she recognized his voice. She then asked him if he was the reporter who had called, and he hung up. He wrote a story stating that there was no such ministry as Circle H Youth Ranch and used my wife's name in the article, and also the name of a trustee implicating him in dishonesty pertaining to the ministry.

The reporter contacted a foundation who had donated to our ministry each year and told them there was no such ministry, and wanted to know why they were making the donation since we did not exist. The reporter also called Dr. James Kennedy's office wanting to know why they supported us, since we were not in existence. The person he talked to told him they knew better because they had been to the facility and saw it with their own eyes. They also knew us personally, and that I had been on Dr. Kennedy's program. The person from Dr. Kennedy's ministry called me right away and told me about the call and informed me that he had called the other foundation.

I took the newspaper article to our State Senator, who was at that time newly elected. He said they had gone too far and a lawsuit needed to be filed to stop it. It seemed that we were finally going to get some action; however, after he talked to some of the older legislators, he decided we did not need to do anything about it. The other legislators had advised him to leave it alone.

It was my understanding that the newspaper reporter lost his job. The newspaper, which was a state paper, could envision a law suit that would be impossible for them to win.

Referring back to the incident I mentioned earlier about having to be in court because my name was added to a lawsuit the state filed against the parents of a former child at the ranch. I arrived at the courthouse that day without an attorney, because I did not have the time to get one, nor the money to pay one. The couple being sued was not there, the child was not there. Only the state attorneys and the Judge. I got there before court convened and told the Judge what had been done and she agreed to let me request a continuance of the hearing in order to get an attorney.

When I walked into the court room and sat down, the two state attorneys were shocked because they didn't expect me to be there.

After the hearing was postponed against the protest of the state attorneys, they told two of our trustees who heard about the hearing and came to the courthouse to be with me, that they had planned to have me held in contempt of court. They didn't think there was any way I could be at the hearing as I was supposed to be in Little Rock at a hearing the state was having.

The hearing was planned specifically for the purpose of trying to put me in jail. I know this because the state attorneys told our trustees that was their intent. They made no secret about their plans to destroy me.

The following is a copy of a letter sent to the Commissioner of Social Services from Governor Frank White. The Commissioner paid no attention to the Governor whatsoever.

Do you understand the consequences of what I am writing? A church has been forced to close. Not a Jim Jones situation, not the occult, not some Eastern religion, but a well known established denomination. This also happened in

America, in the middle of the Bible Belt, not Russia. This is unbelievable and incredible, none the less true. I still find it hard to believe, and want to think that it is all a dream. Believe me, it is not a dream. It has been the most horrible, difficult thing I could ever imagine experiencing.

On one occasion, the state had me scheduled to be in Court in three different counties, the same hour of the same day, knowing I would be in contempt in two counties. The Judge caught this and cancelled two of the hearings.

We have moved from the 160 acre ranch that housed our church, school and childcare facilities. We have sold as many things as we could in order to pay off all the bills that came about because of the attack. We had to turn the deed over to the bank because the mortgage could not be paid. One of the biggest setbacks in something like this, is you lose your support. I guess because many people feel that it will be impossible to start over, or they feel that we wouldn't want to continue after going through all that we have. What many people overlook is, when God calls you to do something, you must do it regardless of the cost. The wonderful thing about it is, God gives the grace and ability to carry on.

I would be less than honest if I didn't say that even though there has been great peace and victory through it all, there has also been times of depression and bitterness. This I had to repent of. It has all been difficult to understand, even though I know the Lord has permitted this to happen, and will do a great work through it according to Romans 8:28, "And we know that all things work together for good to them that love God, to them who are the called according to His purpose". There have been many tears and many unanswered questions. Nothing that happened was a surprise to God. Praise His Name!

While it was a time of scriptural growth and development, it was also a time of spiritual drought. What a contrast! I honestly praise the Lord for all that happened. He is in control. Glory!

I will be traveling for awhile, sharing this story in churches, to help them see the seriousness of what is happening to the church in America. The goal is to close all Christian childcare facilities and Christian Schools and then to control the church and limit what can be preached. We would then no longer have our freedom afforded us by the U.S. Constitution. Many of our freedoms have already been removed in a number of states. I believe the state is wanting to license our Sunday Schools, Visitation Programs, etc. They want to require all Sunday School teachers be state certified teachers. In other words, no one would be able to teach a Sunday School class that was not certified by the state. They could not be certified unless they had a degree in education that qualified them to teach in a public school. We are talking about total control of the church by the state.

I understand there is a town in one of our southern states where it is against the law to have a church of any denomination there. In two cities, in two different states, it is illegal to have a Bible Study in your home. Is this the religious freedom our Constitution guarantees.

I could share many other things that have happened that have infringed upon our religious liberty, but the above will suffice. I have a file full of documented examples. How far are we going to let this matter go? Is God going to have to let the entire church come under total persecution in order to get our attention.

IN THE CHANCERY COURT OF PERRY COUNTY, ARKANSAS

ARKANSAS SOCIAL SERVICES   PLAINTIFF

v.   No. E-82-52

CIRCLE H YOUTH RANCH et al.   DEFENDANTS

ORDER

On the 29th and 30th of July, 1982, came on for hearing plaintiff's request for a preliminary injunction enjoining defendants from operating the Circle H Youth Ranch as an unlicensed child care facility. Plaintiff appeared through the appropriate state officials and counsel, and defendants appeared through authorized representatives, in person, and through counsel. Also appearing was the attorney ad litem appointed by the Court to represent the interests of the children involved. After two days of testimony and evidence and after a review of the pertinent statutes and case law, the Court makes the following findings:

1. Circle H Youth Ranch (herein the Ranch) is an unlicensed child care facility, within the meaning of the Child Care Facilities Licensing Act. The Circuit Court of Pulaski County has upheld the Child Care Facilities Review Board in finding that the Ranch is not entitled to a religious exemption under the statute and, hence, must be licensed to operate.

2. Arkansas Social Services (herein the State) has sought an injunction pursuant to statute enjoining the continued operation of the Ranch as an unlicensed child care facility, both preliminarily and permanently. The case was filed in Perry County, but was tried in Pulaski County on the preliminary injunction request pursuant to Ark. Stat. Ann. 22-407.1.

3. Defendants have maintained that they have the right to operate the Ranch without obtaining a license or exemption, as said operation constitutes free exercise of their religion, under the United States

Constitution. Alternatively, defendants claim that the Court has no jurisdiction to consider the matter, as the enrollment at the Ranch is currently less than six children. To resist the injunction in the face of admitted non-compliance with the statute, the burden is on the defendants to establish the lack of jurisdiction or establish a likelihood of prevailing on the merits on the constitutional issue at the October trial

4. The Court has jurisdiction of the matter, despite the attempt at exemption by reduction of enrollment. The testimony of Rev. Don Grendell established that the designed capacity of the Ranch is for 24 children, and that it would be full, absent this litigation. A temporary reduction in the occupancy of a facility designed for and normally serving well over six children does not exempt it from the statute, any more than a temporary expansion of the occupancy of a small facility would create jurisdiction. Otherwise, jurisdiction could change from day to day, which would not appear to be the legislative intent. Additionally, the essence of the State's request is for a declaratory judgment that the Ranch may not now or in the future operate without a license, which would not require present occupancy of over six children.

5. Most if not all of the children accepted by the Ranch in the last two years have been very difficult to handle. Most have had no meaningful home life or discipline. Physical, mental and emotional problems have been common.

6. All children, and especially these children, have a need for discipline and instruction in values. Despite the State's guidelines, the Court is reluctant to say that corporal punishment in and of itself constitutes abuse, or to say that it is never appropriate. Likewise, the Court does not find that conventional education, as in the public schools, is always appropriate for these children.

7. In almost all instances brought to the Court's attention, it appears that sincere efforts were made to meet the children's needs, on the part of the Ranch staff, Mrs. Brazil and her staff, and by Sheriff

Byrd and his staff. In particular, the Court finds no impropriety on the part of the Sheriff's office in attempting to deal with the children in a protective manner, without the necessity for an arrest record. The Court further finds that no systematic pattern of abuse, neglect or exploitation of the children is established by the evidence.

8. However, the Court does have serious doubts as to whether the Ranch and Rev. Grendell are equipped to adequately deal with the various problems of these children in a meaningful way, in terms of a trained, experienced staff; a comprehensive program of rehabilitation; or an appropriate educational facility, especially for retarded children. In particular, the Court is disturbed and persuaded by Mrs. Rappeport's evaluation of the program, especially the educational aspects. The testimony of Rev. Grendell in fact reinforces rather than dispells these doubts. Even if the Ranch were to close its school program voluntarily, which Rev. Grendell testified that he cannot do, as a matter of faith, the Court is not convinced that the other needs of these children, or others like them, can be met by the Ranch's programs. Though not central to the constitutional issues, the Ranch is not in substantial compliance with the State's published standards, and the school curriculum would not appear to be substantially equal to a public school program, even allowing for the difference in approach inherent in programmed learning.

9. The State of Arkansas has a legitimate interest in enforcing its statutory licensing requirement and the regulations governing child care facilities, for the welfare of the children and to address the special needs of children such as these. The State, by statute, has made provision for the care of children in church-related facilities and, in fact, a wide range of such facilities is available to children and parents seeking such an experience.

10. The Ranch accepts children from a variety of sources, state and private, and for compensation. The Ranch assumes virtually absolute control of the lives of such children. Its position is not the same as that of

parents in a communal setting, such as that of the Amish. The interest of the children in having their needs met and the interest of the State in having those needs met predominate over the interest of the management of the Ranch in their particular perceived free exercise of religion, which necessarily involves others who may or may not have been members of the same community of faith. In particular, the Court is not dealing with a church school whose students body is composed of children of the church's adult members. In fact, Rev. Grendell's perceived ministry, as set forth is his testimony, is to the disturbed and unfortunate child, which of necessity focusses on children outside the church community.

11. Based on these facts, the Court finds Prince v. Massachusetts, 321 U.S. 158 (1944) controlling and persuasive, and finds Wisconsin v. Yoder, 406 U.S. 205 (1972) and Sherbert v. Verner, 374 U.S. 398 (1963) to be useful in providing a necessary distinction in determining that defendants are not likely to prevail on the merits with regard to the constitutional issues at the trial in October.

12. The Court also finds that reassigning three or four students now, before the school year begins, with the possibility that they may be returned to the Ranch, should it prevail at the trial, creates a potential for disruption which is far less serious than would occur were the Ranch to build up its occupancy now, and later have to reassign the students elsewhere to a number of other facilities, were the Ranch not to prevail at trial.

13. The Court finds that the extent of the financial impact on the Ranch is reduced by its income from the chicken operation, the lack of expenses in some areas attributable to the presence of students, and the possibility of continued support through donations.

Based upon these findings, it is hereby

ORDERED, as follows:

A. Any children presently at Circle H Ranch shall be promptly reassigned at the direction of the plaintiff to other appropriate facilities. Defendants shall cooperate in said reassignment, and defendants shall not accept additional children pending a final order herein;

B. The attorney ad litem, Peter Miller, has performed a valuable service to the plaintiff in pursuing the interests of the children involved in this matter and should be paid by the plaintiff the sum of $ 1805 as a fee in this matter, as well as any expenses incurred;

C. Defendants are granted until August 16, 1982, to file an answer;

D. Defendants shall submit a proposed discovery schedule to the plaintiff, through counsel, on or before August 16, 1982;

E. Defendants shall submit to the Court and plaintiff a statement of issues and proposed proof and a memorandum of law on or before August 30, 1982;

F. Plaintiff shall submit any response to said statement and memorandum to counsel for defendants and to the Court on or before September 17, 1982.

W. Christopher Barrier, Special Chancellor

July 30, 1982

STATE OF ARKANSAS
FRANK WHITE
GOVERNOR

August 6, 1982

Mrs. Dorothy K. Rappeport
Commissioner of Social Services
 and Chair of Child Care
 Facility Review Board
P.O. Box 1437
Little Rock, Arkansas 72203

Dear Dorothy:

    It is my decision that the Social Services Division should immediately suspend the involuntary licensure of religious organizations which currently operate residential facilities, day care centers and kindergartens. No administrative or legal actions should be initiated against any such institution until the resolution of the question of separation of church and state, which will be heard in the case of <u>Arkansas Social Services</u> vs. <u>Circle H Youth Ranch</u>, et al.

    I have great concern as to whether the state should require any religiously-sponsored facility to be accredited when we do not have the same requirements in public schools. The regulations on corporal punishment promulgated by the Child Care Facility Review Board are in conflict with laws that specifically authorize such actions in public schools. The fact that public kindergartens are not required to be licensed, and all others are, is also of grave concern to me.

    This directive, in no way, precludes the Agency from investigating any complaints regarding child abuse in any type of facility. However, it is significant to point out that Special Chancellor Chris Barrier found no systematic abuse to any of the children at Circle H, as your agency had alleged.

There appears to be a conflict between Act 63 of 1969, which placed authority for the kindergarten program of this state in the Education Department, and Act 434 of 1969, which provides for the Child Care Facility Review Board to license certain kindergarten programs.

Finally, I have great difficulty with the state interpreting what are "special schools or classes operating solely for religious instruction." Please share with my office those written criteria used by the Child Care Facility Review Board to deny exemption to any religious or church-related facility requesting an exemption because they "operate solely for religious instruction."

When a religious or church-related facility receives no state or federal money, it raises real questions as to why the state should require any type of licensing from them. I plan a very thorough review of our child care and kindergarten licensing requirements to correct these inequities in the future.

Sincerely,

FRANK WHITE
Governor

FW/slc

Chapter 8

How to Stop the Attacks

There is only one way that God can do through His church what He wants to do, and that is when there is total unity. This is not the condition of the church at this time. Denominations do not work together. Even churches within a particular denomination do not work together as they should. My own denomination did not come to me or stand by me during the attack on our ministry. This is so sad, and such a poor witness to a lost and dying world. This is the reason the state can have such a devastating effect on the church. They know we will not stand together, and because of this, they are able to destroy the church, one at a time.

The Bible tells us to "share one another's burdens". Only as we do this and help each other financially can we hope to stand. We have an example of this in the Apostle Paul's day, when the churches took a special offering to help the Church in Jerusalem. If we stick together it might cost each church $100.00 to $200.00; however, when we stand alone, it cost the church between $25,000.00 and $250,000.00. It cost us $100,000.00 as I earlier stated.

Another thing that must be done is for all Christians to get involved with their senators and representatives urging them to pass legislation protecting our churches. The humanists are working very hard to get legislation passed to hinder our churches, and at the present time are doing so with amazing success. How is that possible, you might ask.

It is because Christians are not getting involved in govern-ment. The humanists have convinced most of them that Christians have no place in government positions. The Bible says, "when the righteous rule the people rejoice, and when the unrighteous rule, the people mourn". We have the leaders we deserve because of our lack of' concern and involvement.

A third and very important thing that churches and individuals need to do, is support the Christian Law Association in Cleveland, Ohio. They are God-called attorneys who have dedicated their lives to representing the churches that are being attacked. They do not charge the churches anything for their services. They provide their own travel, lodging, meals and any other personal expenses involved in representing the church. They make tremendous sacrifices; however, they count it a privilege to stand by the churches and pastors. The Christian Law Association represented our church, and I can never thank them enough for all they did. They are some of the finest, most dedicated Christians I have ever had the pleasure of knowing. They are also some of the finest attorneys in our country. There is nothing second rate about any of their staff. They work many long and tedious hours to the Glory of God.

august 2

Dear Mrs Griffin,
How are you? I'm not so good. I want to come back to the ranch so bad, ~~everybody~~ everybody seems to make it sound hopeless, like Ray Brazil and Bill Butler and Judy Balentine. They probably don't mean to make it sound that way. and ~~I~~ when I called Brother Don he made it sound like I might not get to come back. You're the only one that makes me feel good and that I will get to come back soon. I'll try to call you when I get in arkedelphia. I miss everybody at the ranch especially you and brother pete and the Grendells. I cry often everynight and when I think about you and the ranch I cry at least 30 diffrent times a day I'm also crying now. I want to come home so bad I'm almost having a nervous breakdown. Saturaday and today ~~are~~ were the worst days. don't there any way I can come home, please try if there is. I've givens up smokeing and all the bad things I use to do ~~I~~ so the lord can ~~~~ work though me I mean it when I'm able to go back I'm never going to run away or smoke or do anything bad again~~~~ I miss you so much. We went to pettyjean Sunday and pinicle today. but ~~~~ no matter how—

you try its not the same going when your at the ranch. Judy Balentine and another lawyer are going to take me to the movies wensday night. please Mrs Bruffin I'm asking you, no, I'm begging you if there is any possible way to get back before october please do it cause I can't take it any more I need to get back before I have a nervous break down, I'm serious I'm not exaggering I can't take it any more I love you and Brother Pete and I'm so if I've hurt you two in any way cause I do really love you two. please if you can get me back to the ranch

Love
Marc

P.S. excuse the handwriting, pray for me. I love you

Chapter 9

Conclusion

I hope that in some small way I have been able to stir your heart concerning the tremendous problems facing our churches. I further hope and pray that you will be willing to look into the problems further and take a stand before it is too late. Your church could be next.

I firmly believe that if Christians do not begin to stand immediately, the churches in America will begin to face severe persecution. I believe the Lord is trying to warn us in order to keep this from happening. Will you do your part?

If I can help by sharing personally in your church, please feel free to let me know. I believe that the Lord wants to use me in this way to warn churches.

I have had to make a decision to stand on my convictions and face the possibility of jail in doing so, but what less can we do? Jesus paid it all for us, we cannot deny him.

Joshua put it very aptly in Joshua 24:15 "... but as for me and my house, we will serve the Lord".

In conclusion, I have included a copy of a letter from one of the boys we had. The state moved this boy from us against his will. From this, you can see the kind of attitude the children had about our facility.

Won't you pray earnestly that Christian childcare ministries can function without the interference of the state, and these children can have the privilege of knowing Jesus personally. Also, pray for our ministry that we will be able to start our facility again.

May God bless you for your concern. If you would like other books or information on this attack against the church in America, let me know and we will be glad to help you.

Chapter 10

THE ONGOING ATTACK

Well, I thought the book was finished; however, I think the Lord has shown me that it was not the end of the story. I feel I must go back a share a few more details of our experience, as well as share what happened after closing our church and childcare facility.

I have wondered why we could not get the book published, and I guess the reason was, it was not all the story. There is probably no way to share all of it because of the volumes it would take; however, I believe there are some facts that need to be shared.

Part 1

A False Deliverer

One thing we must be careful of in times of trial and tribulation, is an easy way out that Satan might make available.

Just before we had to leave the ranch, there was a person who came into the picture that seemed to be the answer to all our problems. The individual was supposed to be a dedicated Christian and one of wealth. He was going to completely bail us out financially.

The individual was so convincing and could intimidate people to such an extent, that people would do just about anything the person told them to do. So much so, the trustees agreed to turn over all the assets of the ministry, property, buildings, livestock, vehicles and personal property to the individual.

I realized the mistake that was made in doing this and called a special board meeting to rescind their previous action. It goes without saying, that this did not make any points with that person. After a threat was made to me personally, the individual left, never to show up again.

The ironic thing about it all is, Donnie, our son, immediately sensed in his spirit that the person was not for real. However, I played down his cautions because I wanted to believe against hope that it would work out.

We learned first hand the hard way, that the person was not for real. He offered to send us to the Pastor's Conference in Pittsburgh, PA, as well as on vacation, a total of three weeks, all expenses paid. We were given what was supposedly a confirmation by a travel agency that the individual was supposed to own, with all the motel reservations paid in advance. We were to have an Oldsmobile 98 to make the trip in and credit cards for gas and meals. After making all the plans to go, our bags all packed and ready to leave, the car came driving in. It was a compact car. All five of us piled in with our luggage, accepting that as just a little in-convenience. The credit cards were not sent, supposedly forgotten. We were told that would not be a problem, we would be reimbursed when we returned.

Upon arriving at our motel, we discovered that it has not been paid in advance, reservations were not guaranteed. Upon calling and checking into it, we were informed that there had obviously been a mistake and it would be cleared up. It was, when we agreed to put the charge on our Visa card.

When we arrived home, we discovered that nothing was to be reimbursed, and we were now $3,000.00 in debt. Praise the Lord anyway.

We found there were further problems when we got back home. Before leaving, the trustees had agreed to let the individual take the responsibility for getting relief house parents to take care of the children while we were gone. This did not work out either and the trustees took the children into their homes to care for while we were gone.

Another surprise was, we had $250.00 in phone charges made in the name of the ministry. Of course these were to be reimbursed also, just like all the other expenses, and we are still waiting for this reimbursement.

Part 2

Leaving the Ranch

On Labor Day weekend, 1983, we loaded our personal belongings into a rented moving van, and moved into the guest house of one of our trustees. He said we could move in and just pay the utilities. I had no income, but I believed we would soon move to the property that had been donated to the ministry by a friend and continue our ministry.

I was invited to fly to Ft. Lauderdale again to be featured on Dr. James Kennedy's program. I believed the Lord would use this to bring about the financial help we needed.

However, this was another misconception. We never received a single donation or even a letter or phone call as a result of the program. We could not understand why, since we had had such a good response when I was on the program the first time. It was only when we saw the tape of the program that we realized why. The way the program ended, it looked as though we were no longer in the ministry since our church, childcare facility and school were closed. I guess it seemed like it was too late for anyone to help. Nothing was said about us continuing at another location.

Part 3

The Backside of the Desert

I still believed people would help, and as I went into other churches we would get the support we needed. This was another misconception on my part. I started getting calls from churches where I was to preach, cancelling my engagement with them. All of a sudden, I was not preaching anywhere. This was one of the most difficult parts of our entire experience. After being in the ministry for over twenty years, preaching seven to eight times per week, it was a shock to be not preaching at all.

I used to be invited to preach in churches that I would visit from time to time; however, now I found that I might be fortunate just to lead in silent prayer. All of a sudden, no one wanted to be involved in any way. They didn't understand what it was all about and I guess were concerned with what people might say.

Not only was I not getting the opportunity to preach, but I was not even having opportunity to teach or have any part in any of the churches that we belonged to. It didn't matter where we went.

I found myself becoming paranoid and self conscious. I went through a period of bitterness and resentment. It seemed like everyone except my immediate family was against me. I experienced tremendous rejection as a result of this. This was something I had experienced a lot in my childhood, coming from a broken family.

I would read my Bible daily and pray as I always had; however, the Bible just seemed like another book, and there seemed to be no answer to my prayers. It seemed like I was even being rejected by God. This of course, was another one of Satan's lies.

I wanted to go to pastor friends that I thought might be sensitive to what I was going through to try to get their counsel; however, I found that I was lucky to get anyone to agree to spend fifteen minutes with me. They seemed to avoid me like the plague. I was dying inside and wanted someone I could talk to and share my heart, and have them call and pray with me.

There was one layman, Bob Hettinga, that I was introduced to that seemed to understand and became a real friend who welcomed me anytime. I praise the Lord for his compassion and friendship.

It didn't matter what I tried to do, nothing would really come together. I was not even able to make a regular income for my family. The only regular income we had was what Mary earned. This is very hard for a man who had always provided for his family, and in light of what the scripture says about the person who does not provide.

Everything we had was put into the ministry, so we no longer had a home, car, savings, investments or anything of a material value.

We lost all my life insurance in the process, so I had no provision for the family in case of my death.

I began to form the attitude that if that was what my Christian life was going to be, I would rather the Lord call me home and get me out of my misery. I didn't want to leave my wife, children and grandchild, however, I seemed only to be a burden to them. When I considered the possibility of the Lord calling me home, I realized that posed another problem, because I didn't have any way for them to pay for my dying. I was in a terrible predicament, I couldn't afford to live and I couldn't afford to die. Where is the middle ground?

Satan tried to get me to consider suicide and end it all. However, I never could see that as an alternative as a Christian. I think you can see how desperate my situation seemed to be.

Needless to say I experienced a lot of depression and had numerous "pity parties". Each day was just a drudgery to me, with seemingly no purpose and making no progress. I had to repent of all this, knowing that during this time I should have kept my eyes on the Lord and not the problem, and should have been praising Him through it all, rather than complaining and feeling sorry for myself.

Part 4

Someone Who Understood and Was Willing to Help

On one occasion when Mary and I were visiting with her brother, Joe and his wife, Pam; Joe took things into his own hands and took me to see a Christian Counselor, a layman, not a psychologist, a true Christian counselor. We spent many hours together in the weeks and months to come. I began to be able to make some sense of what was going on. It proved to be a real blessing to have someone who understood, cared and would help to find some Scriptural answers to this. It also proved to be a means where I could counsel others in their problems and saw God work some miracles in the lives of others.

I began to understand, at least to some degree, how Satan was deceiving me, and began to deal with some of the rejection of the past. The results were becoming evident to others, even more than to myself.

Through all of this, it made me aware of one of the greatest needs in our churches today, and that is someone who can do Biblical counseling, instead of trying to wrap a cloak of Christianity around secular counseling and calling it Christian counseling. There are so many Christians that are hurting and need help.

One tragic thing that takes place with most Christians, they won't admit they are hurting and need help. People need to learn to be honest.

Part 5

The Lord Provides Encouragement

One of the first things that took place was a deacon from First Baptist Church in Russellville, Arkansas, had a vision of our ministry. He said it was like a big tree that was raised up in the air. It was full grown and was descending back to the ground. In the meantime, the ground under the tree was being broken up and fertilized so the tree would flourish more than ever before. This was showing that our ministry was temporarily suspended and would be reestablished to flourish such as never before.

At a later date, we were invited to a friend's church to hear a singing group. We were strangers to all the others present. About halfway through the service, one of the singers stepped off the platform and singled my wife and I out. She gave a message in tongues concerning our ministry. There was an immediate interpretation. Keep in mind that we were total strangers to the group. The message was that what we had been through was no accident, and we were going to be able to look back in the future and see that our ministry had flourished more than ever before.

On another occasion, I had a person share a word of prophesy with me concerning our ministry. He said that the Lord had permitted the attack for a very special reason and that He was going to restore everything double. He stated that what would happen in our ministry would be so supernatural that everyone would know that it was God's doing.

One of the most supernatural things that happened was one of Mary's bosses (who did not know me personally at that time) stated that one day when he was surveying, the Lord put him on the ground face down and told him to start praying for Don Grendell. As a result of this, we became very good friends and started spending time together. The Lord was revealing to him the same things about our ministry that others had shared previously. The Lord revealed to him that everything we touched would prosper.

We were shown that the attack on our ministry would be for seven years. I am so glad we didn't know that at the beginning of the seven years.

One day I began to reflect on what was happening and it was amazing how things were working out. The Lord had revealed to me through some dreams what was going to happen and then confirmed it with the Scripture concerning Joseph and Pharaoh. We had seven good years at the ranch and the seven year attack on the ministry. The seven years climaxed during my 50th year of life, which also happened to be a Jubilee Year.

Part 6

A Word from the Lord

When the attack started, the Lord revealed to me the outcome of the hearings by a passage of Scripture. He also revealed that we would see our enemies defeated. In other words, the people Satan used to bring the attack on our ministry.

The results were incredible. For instance, during the year that the hearings were going on, six attorneys with the state died, the Commissioner for Social Services resigned, two of the attorneys involved left the state's employment. One of them later committed suicide. Another person was fired, two retired, one with broken health and the Attorney General who was in office during the attack on the ministry, ruined himself politically. One might say these are all coincidences. Well, maybe so, but there were a lot of strange coincidences, wouldn't you say. The only one left who was involved in the attack is President Clinton and he seems to be on rather shaky ground.

We look back with amazement at how God provided over the past seven years, and look forward with excitement to the future and what God is going to do. Praise His Name.

We need your prayers that we might be very sensitive to the Lord's leadership. As I look back, I realize how I have so miserably failed God during this experience. He gave me an opportunity to be a witness for Him that few people have, and I blew it. This was something I had to repent of and I am so thankful that God is so forgiving and gracious. I wonder sometimes why He even puts up with me, but thank God He does.

I hope you appreciate this book and my prayer is that it has been a blessing to you. All the proceeds from the book goes into the ministry to help further the Kingdom of God. Any donation you would care to make will be appreciated. If you would like to know more about Circle H Ministries, please feel free to be in touch with me.

Don Grendell, Th.D.

donbms@suddenlinkmail.com
Circle H Ministry
P.O.Box 1125
Morrillton, Arkansas
72110

www.ingramcontent.com/pod-product-compliance
Lightning Source LLC
Chambersburg PA
CBHW071525180526
45171CB00002B/385